Forbidden Love

Forbidden Love

A Collection of Love Poems

Walter Calvo

iUniverse, Inc.
New York Lincoln Shanghai

Forbidden Love
A Collection of Love Poems

iUniverse books may be ordered through booksellers or by contacting:

iUniverse
2021 Pine Lake Road, Suite 100
Lincoln, NE 68512
www.iuniverse.com
1-800-Authors (1-800-288-4677)

Because of the dynamic nature of the Internet, any Web addresses or links contained in this book may have changed since publication and may no longer be valid.

ISBN: 978-0-595-47180-5 (pbk)
ISBN: 978-0-595-91459-3 (ebk)

Printed in the United States of America

To the Lord, for with

Him all things are possible.

Contents

Foreword

Walter's Calvo's *Forbidden Love* is an extraordinary debut. These tender and compelling poems introduce us to a youth's innocent expression of love. And, in the poet's description of the object of his desire, one is able to feel the essence of the other's presence. The depth of these poems is undeniable and reflects the possibilities that love is meant to offer. Yet the poet's unmasking of the superficiality of love is captured in "Eyes of Sadness." In the poem "Beauty" he unveils the essence of beauty, one that is soulful—a beauty of which we are all capable. The wisdom of Walter Calvo's expression of love is unmistakable and his poems guide us along the journey of what love is really meant to be.

Julie Rainbow, Author
"Standing the Test of Time: Love Stories of African American Elders"

Acknowledgements

I give thanks:

To my parents for encouraging and supporting me in this exciting endeavor.

To my brother, Paul, for his unwavering criticism and support!

To Allyssa for challenging and inspiring me to write. To Carol Hunter for providing creative direction on this project.

To Stacey Moore for tackling the task of copyediting this book.

To Connie Wernersbach for being our "cool" neighbor and for meticulously proofreading this book.

To Kimberly Boykin for her support and promotion services.

Thank you all!

First Glance

My Words that Go Unspoken

These are my words that go unspoken
A realm of beauty yet to be opened–
Your mind is intellectual and kind
You are the most precious treasure I shall ever find
In mine or anyone else's lifetime.
Your eyes are captivating, they astound
Your smile is elegant and profound
Like sunshine without a sound
To you, I'm forever bound.

Wonderful

The colors of your face are like the colors of fall
Joy and beauty contained in all
Your smile is like sunshine indeed
Needed as much as the air I breathe.
Your pretty eyes
Mesmerize
Like stars in the heavenly sky
They shine.
And your mind
Filled with the brilliance of all time
My darling, my beautiful,
You are wonderful.

She Is … Part I

Her beauty is the fire
That my heart desires.
I look into her heart
I see joy, happiness and life
No fear, cruelty or strife.

In her mind
I look, and kindness is what I find
Her intelligence
Is matched only by her brilliance.

Her eyes
Shine like diamonds in the night
She is something I can't define
Her hips are curvaceous as are her lips.

She is beautiful.
And no one can grasp this.
She is …

She Is ... Part II

She is more than you can imagine
She is more stunning than the sunset beyond the mountains
She is lovely.
She is beauty beyond words, nature, and this universe
She is perfect.
She is more than one's eyes should see
She is brilliant.

She is a need, not a want ...
She is everything
She is everyone
She is ...

I Know this Lady

I know this lady who is perfect
Fathom this:
A lady whose eyes luster more than pearls
A lady whose smile makes the roses bloom
A lady who is valued more than the riches of the world
A lady whose hair floats on the wind
A lady whose mind is knowledgeable and pure
A lady who exceeds these very words
A lady amongst our
Goodbyes and hellos …

Miss Elegant Lady

Miss Elegant Lady,
on this special night
Grace follows you
wherever in sight.

To see your smile
to see your beauty
Is worth more to me
than anything.

Your presence sparks
my life and love.

You're an angel with
the purest of
Light and beauty,
and your smile
is radiant all the while.

You are
My beauty,
Miss Elegant Lady.

Miss Graceful

Miss Graceful, how you make me ponder
About your beauty I do wonder
How it exceeds nature's best
I can only guess.

I have never seen beauty in excess,
A delight to every eye
Like a diamond among rubies
Your beauty is no disguise.

I Need

I need you more
I need you less
But less than more can never suppress,
The beating heart within my chest.
Ever since I met you I've felt my best
That's why I can't rest.
Our love,
So wild,
No one can tame …
So solid,
It will never change.
That's why I'm glad you came
Because my life will never be the same …

Within

I can't believe she's trapped in my head!
To my body she's like bread.
She keeps me going why and how?
I need to know
I can't figure this out!
It's not a curse but a wondrous gift
The sight of her helps me live.
I wonder if she knows me, I wonder if she's there
In my thoughts, in the air.
I breathe her out and breathe her in.
Beauty beyond words I'm convinced—
I love her fragrance, it's so sweet
From her head to her feet, she is so lovely.
In my mind, in my heart
She is definitely a part of me.
I wonder silent, I wonder aloud
How can this be?
Everywhere in my soul
Something I indeed
Cannot control.

Masterpiece

Your eyes are like diamonds in the night sky
They shine so magnificently bright
Your hair softly mingles with bare shoulders
Your smile completes me, forever.
Your heart radiates a love so pristine
Your body flows so stunningly
Your mind knows things no one can see ...
You are the one and only masterpiece.

Simply Lovely

Simply lovely
is what you are
Simply lovely
Like a flawless star.

Simply lovely
Are your transpiring eyes
Simply lovely
Like the sunset sky.

Simply lovely
Is your smile
Simply lovely
For all the while.

Simply lovely
Your body is
Simply lovely
With its magnificence.

Simply lovely
Shall you always be
Simply lovely, Simply lovely.

Indescribable

Few words can truly
Describe my thoughts
So I kept thinking …
Then I sought
The ten-pound
College dictionary.
I saw many words
But found none to the contrary.
I referenced
Poe and Hughes,
I listened to
Rhythm and blues.
But I didn't realize
That from the start
All I had to do was
Speak from my heart.
Then I understood it all:

Your beauty is indescribable.

All The World

Yours lips contain a smile
that puts the sun in awe
Your eyes possess a look
that steals the blink from every eye
Your hair carries a fragrance
that smells of sweet September
Your body radiates a beauty
that all desire
Your mind envelops the depth of knowledge,
that compassion so many hope to have
In your heart dwells a love;
a love that is powerful and pure.
You are the world to me
for now, the future, forever and eternity …

All of You

Few words exist to describe you truly
Because you possess beauty so purely.
Your eyes contain brilliant desire
And your smile sets my world on fire.
Your hair falls gently against your shoulder
And your voice warms me all over.
Your presence fills me
With breath so heavenly–
Only you I need
Because,
All of you is beauty.

When I Think of You

When I think of you
I think of your smile
You life expressed
In your style.
Your lovely eyes
Bright and brown
Shine brighter than the sun.
Without a sound
Your hair
Flowing down you back
Smells of roses
And sweet lilac.
These words
Come true
Every time
I think of you.

Love & Beauty

The Beauty of it All

The shine of your eyes
The warmth of your smile
The smoothness of your face
The silkiness of your hair
The tenderness of your lips
The intoxication of your breath

The clasp of our hands.

The intertwining of our hearts.

The depth of our love.

The intensity of the moment
The beauty of you
The beauty of it all …

Beauty Like Grace

I never thought my eyes would find such a masterpiece
Lovely and witty surely are thee
Your elegance envelops my mind
You are truly unique and one of a kind
Like a rose and it's stem
Your beauty and body flow
What more is there to say?
You are beauty like grace.

Beauty

It lies within
Silent and innocent
Sometimes it's not aware that it's living …
Varying in shape and size
Truly and faithfully it is divine.
It may be a secret, it may be a sign
But all know it is one of a kind—
It shows emotion and expression of the mind
It is essential to let it shine …
It, love and comfort are all aligned
Itself, beauty is benign.

Beauty so Rare

You are lovely
there's no doubt in my mind
Your stunning beauty
is truly divine.
Wondrous thoughts
and timeless moments
Foretell the lives
yet to commence …
Captivating eyes
and a heavenly smile,
The essence of beauty
present all the while—
You, my love,
were crafted with
personal care …
Never in my life
have I seen a beauty so rare.

My Beauty

Beauty like yours
No one has ever seen before
Beauty that's cool and free.
Beauty that possesses all desire
Beauty that's uniquely one of a kind
Beauty that defines divine–
The only thing that captivates me is you,
My beauty.

Beauty so Sweet

My feelings are, sincere and true
Everything I love is all that is you
From your wild hair
To your body that's bare
No one else can compare.
Your eyes,
They mystify me.
How could I live without your beauty?
Without your smile to see,
I'd be incomplete
Come close to me,
Beauty so sweet.

My Life and Love

All of myself
All of my life
I put into this simple rhyme
Just to describe your lovely eyes
The way your hair surrounds your face
All of me you captivate
Every time you smile, you lighten my heart
This love won't fall apart—
I know this with all my being
Because witnessing your beauty
Is just like breathing.

I Love

I'd do anything to see
that love in your eyes
all limits of love
we will defy …

I love your mind
I love your style
you brighten my heart
when I see you smile.

All of you
is perfectly
designed to be a part of me;
you're the best life could ever bring.

And for this,
I thank God eternally …

Intimacy

Limitless Love

We lie here together
Just you and I
You in my arms
While I stare into your eyes
Your head rests on my chest.
As I kiss your lips,
Our minds relax.
As we enjoy bliss,
Love brings us together.
Like sand and sun
Your beauty is endless
Like our love, that is limitless …

Midnight Kiss

I'm lying here
with your hand in mine
while tracing the lips of
Your angelic smile.

Your beautiful eyes
(that brilliant brown)
captivates all of me
without a sound.

I taste your sweet breath
and touch your curving hips.
I whisper sweet nothings into your ear.

We close our eyes
and define our bliss.
I pull you closer
and we softly kiss.

Out of bliss
we dive into passion,
our wondrous love
forever lasting.

Your tender body
smooth beneath my fingers.
I move my hand
but your warmth lingers.

Our lips meet once more
and part in a way so shy.

Intimacy

I caress your beautiful face
and we see love eye to eye.

Our hearts come closer
the distance less
and we deeply embrace in this
Midnight Kiss.

Forbidden Love

Footsteps of the heart
echo off the wall
The beauty of the world
and the essence of all.

We embark upon love
against worldly expectation;
Forbidden passions
release a thrilling sensation …

Your seductive eyes
of pure compassion
Hold life
and everything that's happened.

Your lovely smile
amazes beauty yet to come
Your soft, sweet lips
and a kiss is all I've done!

Your natural hair
smells of a fragrant bliss
I'd rather not blink
than a moment of you I miss.

Your satin smooth skin
beneath my fingertips
And the pleasure
that gives way from your lips.

Pure passion
We have stolen from above

Only heightens
This forbidden love.

My Valentine

Three words, not one, not two
These three words say I love you.
I'm here with you on this night
That God created with us in sight.

A bouquet of flowers and chocolate, of course, Given to you my love, conveys so much more ... A beautiful night for us so far As we stand here kissing beneath the stars.

A love like ours could set a fashion
No other love has so much passion.
I treasure this moment in my soul, in my mind For us to revisit, for us to find—

On another year in another way
On another Valentine's Day.

Admiration

A soft light caresses your face
as your hair floats on the wind.
The breeze carries your fragrance
of a sunshine and sweet nectar blend.

Your feet rest upon the sand
which they so gently cradle
The radiance from your body
provides more warmth than a million candles.

Your brilliant eyes scan the horizon
as yellow sun turns white moon.
Your smile embraces nature's magnificence from morning until midnight moon.

You lie there now
letting all nature admire
As your presence
makes the moons shine brighter and brighter.

Heart of Gold

I want to know you
Better than I know myself.
I want to be
The air you breathe.

I want to hold you
So close in my arms,
I want to be the one to protect you from harm.
I want it to be your eyes that I stare into at night.

I want to caress your beautiful face,
Kiss your lips,
Hand in your hand and hand on your hips.

All the while
We lay there with a smile,
Because we are with each other,
Forever, together.

This is the first time its you I told,
I want to polish your heart of gold.
Gold can barely
Express the kind of heart I see,
With a mind so perfectly
Wrapped up in a wonderful frame.

Beauty is your name.

Come Away

There you are my Darling
I've been waiting for you,
Come away with me
On this new journey.
Happiness will surround you
And love will abound between us two!
Your beautiful eyes will never see a day of gloom
Ever since the sweet blossoms bloom,
From the spring to the fall
You have it all.
Place your hands in mine,
And let's love, for a lifetime.

Forever Yours

Your delicate hands are safe in mine

I ask one quiet question: will you be mine?

A smile of an angel's and the twinkle in your eye Reveal your answer to me tonight.

Lights, people, but only us by chance

In the midst of them all, we begin to dance

The thought of our hearts shared all along

We hold each other, listening to most romantic of songs.

Your eyes of deep desire show me true bliss

Your tender lips taste sweet as we kiss

I am forever yours, and you are forever mine—

Love was ours, on this Valentine's.

When I and You

When I gaze into your eyes,
I am mesmerized by your beauty.
When I look at your hair,
I see your curls so lovely, so rare.
I love your smile, so stunning and sweet;
Your presence makes me totally complete.
Your body so slender and lean,
Your walk graceful, your mind keen.
Truly you are the most beautiful thing I have ever seen.
And I can't wait to hold you close to me.

Sapphire Lightning

Sitting in front of night's warm fire
Your softly lit eyes posses my desire.
A blue wonder ye to know
A sapphire lightning that my eyes hold.

Words of you, me, and midnight bliss
Wrapping my arms around you, worries amiss.
Our love intimately imitates the fire
The heat of the moment sending us higher and higher …

Your hair floats delicately in the night As you turn around and begin to smile The air is in our love, our hearts know this Your tender lips I gently kiss.

Our love grows brighter as all else wanes Rising into the night as do the flames.
You are my angel, my only one
You are the lady I love.

Moonlight

The sun has set
and the moon watches over us.
Our fingers interlock
and we are all that was …
Your lips tease mine
searching for bliss,
I pull you close
and we kiss.
Your delicate lips taste of passion,
We embrace
this moment everlasting.
We forget tomorrow
and yesterday;
time stands still
as intimacy gives way.
Your body against mine feels right,
truly this is bliss under moonlight.

Empty Love

Tear Drop

A glistening tear drop rest on her eye,
A soft kiss began the lie.
A soothing touch and a warm grasp,
Started the questions to ask.
A birth of life between them
Initiated all the hurt that came from him.

The tear drop falls, but lands not on the floor Another is there to ask once more.
Burden by the worries of her yesterday,
She sets sail never to return again.
As her journey goes on and on,
She lets go and ceases the mourn.
Another birth comes from this journey
That of her spirit controlled by her heartbeat.

The tear drop now abandoned
Lies alone empty-handed.
Until another comes to find
Love's weary alibi.
Once again like fate she falls
And another heart is there to call;
Just to ask another question.
Surely the pain is there to lessen
Everything felt with inside.
With nothing left to hide,
The birth of fear
Returns once more here.

Although the tear drop visited another,
It would not steal away forever.
Maybe in another form, another state

Intrigued by love or by hate
Not long now until a day goes by
And a glistening tear drop rests on her eye.

Eyes of Sadness

Her eyes pierce the heart
Of strongest resistance.
Thousands of words spoken
But none with magnificence.

Hopeful reassurance
But everlasting mistake;
No matter what is said
Happiness she can never take.

There is no love,
Only madness;
all she sees is pain
With those eyes of sadness.

Receded in the shadows
Her soul is shown now,
Why must her eyes
Always look down?

Burden with troubles
All the while,
It helps
Just to smile.

Walk and look at me
With your grace.
See me eye to eye
Feel my embrace;

And let this,
Heal your eyes of sadness.

Love's Trilogy

In Your Smile

You, my love,
Possess an uncontrollable beauty—
Your presence
Enlightens me.

Dreams are no more
Because we both can see
Our love has become a reality.

Our eyes locked in
Each other's hearts
I knew we were meant to be
From the very start.

The way you kiss
My lips tonight,
Every part of me
Was electrified.

My fingers gently touching your face so smooth,
Planning not, our next move
Letting the mood lead us through …

The two of us
Interlocked together
Both our hearts
Beating forever.

Love will surely
Keep us here a while. This is foretold in your smile.

Lay Your Head

Lay your head on my chest
take a slow deep breath
Exhale, and let all rest …

Look in my eyes
you can see our love
The purest of all
and it's because
Of you.

Here, just us two
collecting all that went amiss
against this moment we softly kiss;
Closed eyes we enjoy bliss …
While we're shrouded in love's mist.

Your hands on my back and my fingers through your hair Our lips give way to an
experience so rare.

I feel your smooth skin on mine
As we both sense this moment divine.

We kiss one last time
on this special night
Taking slow deep breaths
As you lay your head …

True Love's Confession

Hold my hand
my beauty queen
Stare into my eyes
tell me what you see.

Let me breathe you
in and out.
Let me cleanse you
withal and throughout.

Let's kiss right now
in this moment
We will be together
everyday forever spent.

We are intertwined in love
and combined in heart
Laying together
we will never be apart.

With you in my soul
and me in your mind
We will create a love
no words can define.

Your eyes control our rhythm
and our pace,
My love controls our harmony
and our embrace.

We surrender to intensity
As all inhibitions are let go,

Love controls us
As intimacy flows.

I and all of you,
You and all of me,
Intertwined together
For all eternity.

Through fiery passion
We hear the echo of
True Love's Confession ...

978-0-595-47180-5
0-595-47180-3